THE PSYCHE - GOD WITHIN

Uncovering the Hidden Universal Truth

NIVIN RAVI

ISBN
Paperback 979-8-89610-774-3
Hardcase 979-8-89699-918-8

Dedication

In the Name of God

To my beloved wife, Reshma, for your unwavering love, support, and belief in me, you are my constant inspiration and source of strength.

To my dear children, Aidan and Aura, may you always walk the path of love and wisdom, and discover the divine truth within yourselves.

This journey is as much yours as it is mine.

With all my heart, I dedicate this work to you.

Thank you to all the people and lives that I have come across and the ones

Yet to come across in this lifetime…

Contents

The Forgotten Garden 🌿 ✦

"**B**efore we knew fear, we were whole. Before we were broken, we were divine. Before we forgot, we were love."

There was once a time— before the fractures, before the masks, before the layers of stories— when we lived in perfect harmony. Not in the world outside, but within. A sacred garden, untouched and pure, where the soul danced freely, unbound by fear, unmarked by time. This was the Psyche within— the place where love wasn't something we sought, but something we were.

But somewhere along the way, we forgot.

The Fall into Forgetting 📖 💔

The forgetting wasn't sudden. It happened in whispers— in moments of pain too deep to bear, in words unspoken, in love withheld. 💡 A child laughed… but was told to be quiet. 💡 A heart broke… and was taught to harden. 💡 A dream sparked… but was buried beneath "reality."

Piece by piece, we closed the gates to the garden within. We built walls— to protect, to survive, to fit in. But in doing so, we abandoned the very essence of who we were. And so, we wandered. Searching for love in others, seeking validation in the world, chasing wholeness in fragments. All the while, the garden within remained— waiting, calling, whispering, 💡 "Remember me."

The Cracks That Let the Light In ✸ 🌿

But the soul has a way of breaking through. In the moments when the pain becomes too much, when the masks grow too heavy, when the noise quiets just enough— 💡 We feel it.

- A flicker of truth.

- A surge of emotion.

- A memory… not from the mind, but from the soul.

The garden calls out, and for a brief moment, the walls crack, and light seeps through. This is where the journey begins— not in becoming someone new, but in remembering who we've always been.

The Journey Home 🪶 🌙

This is the story of that remembering. Of two souls—Numan and Sophia— who, like all of us, forgot the truth of who they were. Their journey is not unique. It is the journey of humanity— from fragmentation to wholeness, from fear to love, from forgetting to awakening. Through their struggles, their pain, their breakthroughs— you will see reflections of yourself. Because this story isn't just theirs— 💡 It's yours. A call to return. A path back to the Psyche within. A remembrance that you were never broken. Never lost. Never separate. You were always whole. You were always love. You only forgot. But now, dear reader, 💡 it's time to remember. 📖 💗

Chapter 1

The Garden of Love 🌿

Before the Fall, There Was Only Love

We are all born into a garden. Not one of flowers and trees, but of pure presence— where love flows freely, where laughter echoes without shame, where the soul remembers its infinite nature. This garden is untouched by fear, unmarked by judgment, unbroken by the world's expectations. 💡 In this garden, we are whole.

But slowly—almost imperceptibly— the world teaches us something different. It whispers:

- "You must earn love."

- "You are not enough as you are."

- "Hide your truth, or you will be rejected."

And so, the garden begins to fade, overgrown with weeds of fear, walls rising where once there was openness. This is where the story begins— with two souls who, like all of us, once lived in that garden and then forgot.

Numan: The Silent Seeker 📖 🍀

As a child, Numan saw the world through eyes wide with wonder.

- The wind wasn't just air—it was a song.

- The stars weren't just distant lights—they were whispers of infinity.

- His heart wasn't just a muscle—it was a compass, always pointing toward love.

But even in this purity, the cracks began to form early. His father, a man burdened by expectations and unhealed wounds, believed love was something to be earned— through discipline, achievement, and control. ♀ "Boys don't cry." ♀ "Be strong. Don't be soft."

These words, spoken in love but steeped in fear, echoed through Numan's young heart, turning his open garden into a place of caution. He learned to smile when he was sad, to nod when he disagreed, to stay silent when his heart screamed. ♡ "If I am perfect, I will be loved."

And so, the first wall was built— a barrier between his true self and the version of himself he believed the world wanted. But deep beneath the surface, the garden still lived, waiting to bloom again.

Sophia: The Fragile Bloom ❀ ♡

Sophia's childhood was filled with beauty and chaos, a delicate dance between love and absence. Her mother was a force— graceful, poised, and endlessly striving for perfection. But her love often felt conditional, woven with expectations.

- "You're my little star, but stars must shine bright."
- "Good girls don't make mistakes."

Sophia became a master of performance—

- Smiling even when her heart ached.
- Achieving to feel worthy.
- Hiding her softness to be strong.

She felt the weight of needing to be "enough" but could never quite grasp what that meant. ♡ "If I'm perfect, I'll be seen. If I'm flawless, I'll be loved."

Her garden, once vibrant and wild, became manicured— each flower pruned, each vine controlled, until only an illusion of beauty remained. But like Numan, deep within her soul, the original garden still pulsed, longing to break free.

The Illusion of Love 💔 🖼

Both Numan and Sophia grew up believing that love was conditional— something to be earned, chased, or controlled. They didn't realize that the love they sought had never truly left. ♀ It was buried beneath the masks. ♀ Hidden beneath the fears. ♀ Waiting patiently in the forgotten garden within.

But life has a way of bringing us back— through cracks in the walls, through moments of pain, through the soft whispers that call us home.

The First Cracks ⚡ 🌿

For Numan, it was a moment of quiet rebellion— standing beneath the old oak tree in his backyard, tears streaming down his face after another scolding from his father. 💬 "Why can't I just be me?"

The thought came uninvited, but it was the first crack in his wall. For Sophia, it was a simple moment— watching a butterfly land on a flower and realizing that the butterfly didn't have to earn its place, didn't have to prove its worth. 💬 "Why do I?"

That single thought stirred something deep within her— a flicker of truth beneath the years of conditioning.

The Call to Remember ✳ 🗯

The journey back to the Psyche within doesn't begin with clarity. It begins with a question— a soft whisper that challenges the illusions we've built our lives upon. For Numan and Sophia, the cracks had begun. And through them, the first beams of light pierced the darkness. The garden had not been destroyed. It had only been forgotten. ♀ And now, it was calling them home. 🖼 💗

Chapter 2

The Conditioning and Family Tree 🌳 💔

We Inherit More Than Blood—We Inherit Stories
Before we even speak our first words, before we understand love or fear, we inherit something deeper— The stories of those who came before us.

- Stories of strength and survival.

- Stories of love and loss.

- Stories of fear disguised as protection.

These stories flow through us like roots beneath the surface— invisible, yet powerful. They shape how we love, how we see ourselves, how we navigate the world. 💡 We do not just inherit genetics; we inherit wounds. And until we see them, we unknowingly live them, passing them down like branches on a family tree.

Numan: The Roots of Control 📖 🌳

Numan grew up under the heavy branches of expectation. His father, Adil, was a man of few words— stoic, disciplined, and burdened by his own unspoken wounds.

- Adil believed that love was shown through provision, not emotion.

- That discipline was strength, and vulnerability was weakness. 💡 "Be a man. Control yourself."

These words echoed through Numan's childhood, weaving themselves into his identity. Every time he cried, his father would sigh deeply, "Tears won't fix anything. Toughen up."

So Numan learned.

- He learned to suppress his emotions.
- He learned that love was tied to success.
- He learned that control equaled safety.

But beneath the surface, the boy who longed to run free, to laugh without fear, to cry without shame— still existed. Buried beneath layers of conditioning, waiting to be remembered.

Sophia: The Fractured Mirror

Sophia's family tree was tangled with contradictions. Her mother, Elena, was a picture of grace and poise— always composed, always "perfect." But behind that polished exterior was a woman carrying generations of unhealed wounds.

- Elena was taught that worthiness came through beauty and achievement.
- That vulnerability was dangerous, and emotions were messy. "You're my little star, but you have to shine bright."

Sophia grew up trying to meet those expectations.

- She became the "good girl"—polite, obedient, always striving.
- She excelled in school, in dance, in everything she touched.

But inside, she felt a growing emptiness. "If I stop performing, will I still be loved?"

This silent question followed her like a shadow, haunting her brightest moments, reminding her that love felt conditional— always just out of reach.

The Inherited Wounds 💔 🌿

Both Numan and Sophia carried the weight of their family trees—

- Unspoken traumas.

- Conditioned beliefs.

- Generational patterns passed down without question.

They didn't choose these stories. But they lived them.

- Numan lived the story of control— believing that only by holding everything together could he be worthy of love.

- Sophia lived the story of perfection— believing that only by being flawless could she be seen and accepted. 💡 These weren't their stories. But they had become their identities. And like many of us, they didn't even realize it.

The Invisible Chains 🔗 📱

The most powerful chains are the ones we can't see. They're woven into the way we speak, the way we love, the way we fear. They whisper in the background:

- "You're not enough."

- "You must earn love."

- "Don't be too much. Don't be too little."

These beliefs, passed down through generations, become invisible scripts, guiding our every move until we decide to question them. For Numan and Sophia, the questioning hadn't come yet. But the cracks had begun.

The Moment of Awareness 🌸 🌿

Awareness often begins in small moments— fleeting, fragile, but powerful. For Numan, it was a simple memory. He watched his father scold his younger brother, using the same words that had once been aimed at him. 💡 "Don't cry. Be a man."

But this time, instead of agreement, Numan felt something different— Pain. He saw the cycle repeating— unquestioned, unbroken. And in that moment, a thought surfaced: 💬 "What if there's another way?"

For Sophia, her moment came while flipping through an old family photo album. She noticed something striking— in almost every picture, her mother's smile was perfect, but her eyes were distant, guarded. Sophia touched the photo, feeling a surge of emotion. 💬 "Has she been performing too? Just like me?"

It was the first time she saw her mother not as the authority figure, but as a woman carrying her own unhealed wounds. And for the first time, Sophia felt compassion— for her mother, and for herself.

The Seed of Liberation 🌱 💞

These moments didn't shatter the walls or break the chains completely. But they planted seeds— tiny, fragile, but full of possibility. 💡 The seed of awareness. The first step toward liberation is seeing the chains that bind us.

- Not with anger.
- Not with blame.
- But with compassion.

Because the wounds we inherit aren't anyone's fault. They're passed down from generation to generation— not out of malice, but out of survival. 💡 "We carry the pain we didn't know how to heal." But we also carry the power to break the cycle.

The Family Tree Transformed 🌳 ✦

Imagine a family tree, its roots tangled with generations of pain, its branches heavy with expectations. But then— someone plants a new seed. A seed of love. Of awareness. Of healing. And over time, new branches grow— ones that reach toward the sun, unburdened, free. 💡 This is what Numan and Sophia had unknowingly begun. The journey of healing doesn't just free us— it frees everyone connected to us. When we heal, we heal forwards and backwards— transforming not just our own lives, but the lineage we came from and the generations yet to come.

Closing Reflection: Questioning the Stories 💡 🌳

We all carry stories that aren't ours.

- Beliefs inherited without question.

- Wounds passed down like heirlooms.

- Fears disguised as protection.

But the beauty of awareness is that it gives us a choice. 💡 "Do I continue this story? Or do I write a new one?"

Numan and Sophia had taken the first step— not by breaking the chains completely, but by seeing them. And in that seeing, the journey toward freedom had truly begun. 📒 🤍

Chapter 3

The Masks We Wear 🎭💔

W e Build Them to Survive—But They Keep Us From Living
Somewhere along the path of growing up, we begin to hide. We
cover our hearts with layers of protection—masks crafted from fear,
expectations, and the deep desire to be loved.

- A mask of strength to hide the fear.

- A mask of perfection to hide the shame.

- A mask of indifference to hide the longing.

💡 We believe these masks will protect us. But over time, they become
cages. They separate us from who we truly are—from our vulnerability,
our joy, our wholeness.

This is the story of how Numan and Sophia forgot themselves
beneath their masks and how, eventually, the masks began to crack.

Numan: The Mask of Control ✂️📋

Numan's mask was built from the belief that control equalled safety.
He became the one who had it all together—the achiever, the strong
one, the one who never faltered.

- He excelled in school, pushing himself to the limit.

- He buried his emotions deep, believing vulnerability was
  weakness.

- He became the caretaker, constantly ensuring others were
  okay—even when he wasn't.

But beneath the mask, a storm brewed. He felt the weight of his own expectations crushing him, but he refused to let it show. 💬 "If I let go, everything will fall apart."

Yet, late at night, alone in his room, the cracks would appear—

- Silent tears shed into his pillow.

- A deep, aching loneliness that he couldn't explain.

- A whisper within, asking, "Is this really who I am?"

But the next morning, the mask would return, polished and perfect, ready to face the world.

Sophia: The Mask of Perfection ✿ 🎭

Sophia's mask was one of perfection—a carefully crafted image of the flawless daughter, the ideal friend, the high achiever. She learned early that being "good" earned her love and approval.

- Straight A's in school.

- A perfect smile in every photo.

- A life that looked beautiful on the outside.

But inside, she felt hollow. 💬 "If they saw the real me, would they still love me?"

She couldn't remember the last time she had allowed herself to simply be—without performing, without striving, without proving her worth. Her emotions were tightly controlled, her true self buried beneath layers of "should" and "musts."

But the cracks in her mask began to form in the quiet moments—

- When she stood alone in her room, exhausted from trying so hard.

- When she felt a surge of anger or sadness, only to immediately suppress it.

- When she saw a child laughing freely and felt a pang of longing for that same freedom.

Her mask was beautiful—but it was suffocating her.

The Purpose of Masks 💡 🕯

We don't wear masks because we're weak. We wear them because, at some point, they kept us safe.

- Numan's mask of control protected him from rejection.
- Sophia's mask of perfection shielded her from the fear of not being enough.

💡 Masks are survival tools. But over time, what once protected us begins to imprison us. We become trapped in the very identities we created to be loved. And the deepest wound of all? 💡 We start believing the mask is who we really are.

The Moment the Mask Cracks ⚡ 💔

For Numan, the crack appeared during a business presentation—his carefully crafted pitch fell flat, and the client rejected his ideas. His heart pounded, his mind raced, and for the first time in years, he felt something terrifying: 💡 Powerlessness.

He had built his entire life around control, but in that moment, he realized he couldn't control everything. A voice inside whispered, 💬 "Who am I without this mask?"

The question lingered, planting the first seed of doubt.

For Sophia, the crack came during a family dinner. Her mother praised her achievements, listing them one by one—but Sophia felt no pride, only emptiness. Her younger cousin, innocent and free, looked at her and asked, 🗣 "Are you happy?"

The question pierced through her armour. Her throat tightened, tears welled up, but she smiled through it, 💡 "Of course." But deep down, she knew the truth— 💬 "I don't even know what happiness feels like anymore."

The Weight of Inauthenticity ⚖ 💔

Wearing a mask is exhausting. It requires constant vigilance, endless energy, and the suppression of our most authentic selves. Both Numan and Sophia felt the heaviness of living out of alignment—of being seen, but not truly known. 💡 "How long can I keep this up?"

This is the silent question that so many carry, hidden beneath the layers of their identities.

The Call to Remove the Mask ♻ 💡

The journey back to the Psyche within begins when the mask starts to crack—when the weight of inauthenticity becomes too heavy to bear. But removing the mask isn't easy. It requires:

- Courage to face the parts of ourselves we've hidden.
- Compassion for the wounded child who built the mask in the first place.
- Trust that who we are beneath it is already enough.

For Numan and Sophia, the cracks had formed. And through them, the first glimpses of their true selves began to emerge—

- Messy.
- Raw.
- Real.

💡 "What if who I really am is worthy of love?"
It was a terrifying thought. But it was also their first step toward freedom.

Closing Reflection: The Masks We All Wear 🎭 🌿

We all wear masks.

- To be loved.
- To be accepted.
- To survive.

But the path to awakening is the path of removing them—gently, compassionately, and without shame. 💡 Because beneath the mask is the real you—the you who is already whole, already enough, already love.

Numan and Sophia had begun this journey. And now, dear reader, perhaps the question is: 💡 "What mask am I still wearing? And who am I beneath it?" ✒ 💗

Chapter 4

The Awakening Storm 🌪️ 💔

The Storm Doesn't Destroy You—It Destroys What's False

There comes a moment on every journey when the walls we've built can no longer hold. The masks crack. The lies unravel. The storm begins. And though we fear it, though we run from it, 💡 the storm doesn't come to break us—it comes to break what isn't truly us.

For Numan and Sophia, the storm was no longer on the horizon. It was here.

Numan: When Control Slips Away 🗡️ 📖

Numan had always prided himself on being in control.

- His emotions? Locked away.
- His life? Meticulously planned.
- His image? Flawless.

But control is an illusion. And illusions eventually shatter. It started small—missed deadlines, strained relationships, sleepless nights filled with anxiety. But the moment the storm truly hit came during a presentation at work. His boss criticized his project in front of the team, dismissing months of effort with a few sharp words. Numan's chest tightened. His hands trembled. But he smiled, nodded, and pretended it didn't sting. 💬 "Hold it together. You can't fall apart now."

But inside, something cracked. That night, alone in his apartment, the dam finally broke. He fell to his knees, tears streaming down his

face—raw, uncontrollable, years of suppressed pain flooding out. ☿
"I'm so tired of holding it all together."

In that moment, he realized the truth— ☿ Control hadn't protected him. It had imprisoned him. And now, the walls were collapsing.

Sophia: When Perfection Fails ❀ 🎭 💔

Sophia had built her identity on being perfect.

- Perfect grades.

- Perfect smiles.

- Perfect life.

But perfection is a fragile house of cards, and the wind had begun to blow. Her breaking point came during her best friend's wedding. Surrounded by people, laughter, and beauty—she felt… nothing. No joy. No connection. Only emptiness. 💭 "Why can't I feel anything? What's wrong with me?"

During the reception, she slipped away to the bathroom, locking the door behind her. She looked at her reflection—the flawless makeup, the carefully styled hair, the perfect mask—and suddenly, it felt unbearable. She gripped the sink, tears welling in her eyes, and whispered, ☿ "I don't know who I am anymore."

The truth hit her like a wave— ☿ Perfection hadn't made her lovable. It had made her invisible. And in that moment, the mask shattered.

The Nature of the Storm ⚱ ☿

The storm isn't just chaos. It's the awakening force that rips away the false layers so the truth can emerge. ☿ It feels like destruction, but it's actually creation.

Both Numan and Sophia were now in the centre of their storms—their identities unravelling, their illusions breaking apart. It was terrifying. But it was also the beginning of their freedom.

The Gift Hidden in the Pain 💔 🎁

Pain often feels like punishment. But in truth, it's a messenger.

- Numan's pain wasn't about failure—it was about the years he'd abandoned himself in the name of control.

- Sophia's emptiness wasn't a flaw—it was the result of a life spent performing rather than living.

💡 The storm showed them what they could no longer ignore. And within that pain, a new voice began to emerge—quiet, fragile, but persistent. 💬 "There's more to you than this."

The Moment of Surrender 🐘 ❄️

The turning point in every storm isn't when we fight harder—it's when we finally surrender. Not in defeat, but in acceptance.

- Numan, sitting on his living room floor, allowed himself to cry—fully, openly—for the first time in years.

- Sophia, still in the wedding bathroom, wiped away her tears, but not her emotions. She didn't "fix" herself. She just… felt.

💡 Surrender isn't giving up. It's letting go of what no longer serves us. And in that space, something new can be born.

The Eye of the Storm 🌪️ ✦

In the centre of every storm is a place of stillness—the eye.

- Numan, amidst his breakdown, felt a strange peace settle over him. He wasn't okay, but he was real.

- Sophia, amidst her tears, felt a flicker of truth—a glimpse of the self she had buried beneath all the layers.

💡 This was the eye of their storms—the place where the false falls away and the authentic begins to emerge.

The Awakening Begins ✳ ♡

The storm doesn't end everything. It begins everything.

- It awakens what's been dormant.

- It frees what's been trapped.

- It calls us back to the Psyche within.

For Numan and Sophia, this was the true start of their journeys—the moment they realized they could no longer live the way they had. 💡 The storm had broken them open, but through those cracks, the light was beginning to pour in.

Closing Reflection: Embracing the Storm 🌪 💡

We all face storms—moments when life tears away the illusions we've clung to. And while it feels like breaking, it's actually a form of healing. 💡 "The storm isn't here to destroy you. It's here to destroy what isn't really you."

Numan and Sophia had entered the storm. And now, they had a choice—

- Rebuild the walls.

- Or step into the unknown and finally meet their true selves.

The journey deeper into the Psyche within had truly begun. 🪨 ♡

Chapter 5

The Dark Night of the Soul ☻ 💔

Before the Dawn, There Is Darkness
The path to awakening is not a straight line. It twists. It turns. It descends into shadows before reaching the light. 💡 "To find the soul, we must first lose ourselves."

This descent is known as The Dark Night of the Soul—a place where everything familiar dissolves, where the masks have fallen, but the true self has not yet emerged. It is a void. A silence. A darkness so deep, it feels endless. But it is also the place where rebirth begins.

Numan: The Hollowing Out 📖 ⚫

After the storm, Numan expected relief. But instead, he found emptiness. Days blurred together. Tasks that once felt important now felt meaningless. He sat at his desk, staring at a glowing screen, unable to move, unable to care. 💭 "Who am I without all of this?"

His identity—the achiever, the caretaker, the controlled—had cracked and fallen away. But beneath it, there was... nothing. No purpose. No passion. Only a vast emptiness echoing through him.

He stopped answering calls. Stopped replying to emails. Even friends noticed the shift— 🗣 "Are you okay?"

But how could he explain the ache inside? 💡 "I'm not who I thought I was. But I don't know who I am now."

This was the hollowing out—the painful space between identities, where the false has fallen away, but the true has not yet been found.

Sophia: The Disconnection ✿ ⬤

Sophia found herself in a similar void. After the wedding breakdown, she tried to return to normal—to the routines, the perfection, the performance. But everything felt... off.

- Conversations felt shallow.

- Achievements felt empty.

- Even her own reflection felt like a stranger.

She spent hours scrolling through social media, watching others live "perfect" lives, feeling more disconnected with every swipe. 💬 "Was I ever really happy? Or was I just pretending all along?"

The realization hit her hard—most of her life had been a performance, and now that the mask was cracking, she didn't know how to be real. Tears came easily, but they didn't bring relief. 💡 "I feel lost. Like I'm floating with no anchor."

This was her dark night—a space of profound disconnection, where even her own heart felt distant.

The Nature of the Dark Night 🌑 💡

The Dark Night of the Soul feels like death. And in many ways, it is—the death of who we thought we were.

- It strips away the false identities.

- It exposes the wounds we've buried.

- It leaves us naked, vulnerable, and raw.

💡 "The dark night is not a punishment. It is a purification."

But in the midst of it, all we feel is the emptiness—the terrifying void where everything we clung to has been ripped away.

The Isolation 🗡 💔

One of the cruellest illusions of the dark night is the belief that we are alone in it. Both Numan and Sophia felt this isolation deeply—

- Numan, sitting alone in his apartment, surrounded by walls that echoed his loneliness.

- Sophia, lying in bed, scrolling through messages she didn't have the energy to answer.

💬 "No one understands this. No one sees me."

But the truth is—so many have walked this path. So many are walking it now. 💡 "The dark night feels isolating, but it connects us all in our most vulnerable state."

It is the universal journey of the soul—the breakdown before the breakthrough.

The Surrender 🌀 ✦

The turning point in the dark night doesn't come from fighting it. It comes from surrender.

- Numan, after weeks of numbness, finally sat on his floor, hands open, tears streaming down his face, and whispered, 💡 "I don't know who I am anymore. But I'm willing to find out."

- Sophia, staring at her reflection, placed her hand over her heart and for the first time in her life, didn't criticize herself. 💡 "I don't know how to be me. But I want to try."

These moments of surrender are the flickers of light in the darkest night. They signal the soul— 💡 "I'm ready to return."

The Light Hidden in the Darkness ✳ ⚉

The dark night feels endless, but it holds within it the seeds of awakening.

- In the emptiness, we find space for truth.

- In the disconnection, we realize the depth of our longing for authenticity.

- In the silence, we hear the whispers of the Psyche within.
  💡 "The darkness is not the end. It is the womb of the new self."

Both Numan and Sophia, though still lost, had taken their first steps toward the light. Not by climbing out, but by sinking deeper into themselves—into the spaces they had long avoided.

Closing Reflection: The Gift of the Dark Night ● ♡

If you are in the darkness now, know this— ♀ "The dark night is not where you are lost. It is where you are found."

It is brutal. It is lonely. It feels endless. But it is also sacred. Because when everything else falls away—the masks, the identities, the expectations—what remains is you. Raw. Real. Whole. ♀ "The dawn always follows the darkest night. But first, you must sit in the stillness and remember who you truly are." ▨ ♡

Chapter 6

Meeting the Inner Child 👦🐣

The Parts We Abandon Are the Ones That Hold the Key to Our Wholeness

We are all born whole—

- Pure, innocent, and radiant. But somewhere along the way, we begin to fracture.
- The playful parts are silenced.
- The sensitive parts are shamed.
- The wild, free parts are tamed. 💡 "To survive, we abandon the very parts of ourselves that make us feel most alive."

But they never truly leave. They wait— deep within the Psyche, in the forgotten corners of our hearts— for the moment we are ready to return to them.

This is the journey of meeting the inner child— the wounded, hidden self that holds both our deepest pain and our purest joy.

Numan: The Boy Who Was Never Enough 📖 👦

Numan sat on his apartment floor, surrounded by the silence that had become deafening. The dark night had stripped him bare, and now, there was only emptiness. 💬 "Who am I without control? Without achievement?"

He closed his eyes, letting the stillness take over. But then— a memory surfaced.

- A younger version of himself, no more than seven years old, sitting alone in his room, clutching a toy soldier. His father's angry voice echoed in the background. 🗣 "Stop crying. Be a man."

The boy tried to hold back tears, but they spilled anyway, silent and desperate.

Numan's chest tightened. He watched this memory as if it were unfolding in real time. 💡 "That's me. That's the part I left behind."

His heart ached. He knelt beside the image of his younger self, tears streaming down his face. 💡 "I'm so sorry I left you alone."

The boy looked up, eyes wide with sadness and hope. 💬 "I just wanted to be loved."

In that moment, Numan felt a surge of emotion— an overwhelming compassion for the child within him. He reached out, gently holding the boy, whispering, 💡 "You didn't have to be perfect. You were always enough."

And as he said the words, he realized— they weren't just for the boy. They were for himself.

Sophia: The Silenced Dreamer 🌸 👧

Sophia lay curled on her bed, the weight of the dark night still heavy. She had tried meditating, journaling— anything to ease the emptiness. But nothing worked. Until she heard it— a soft, distant sound, like a child's laughter echoing in the wind.

She closed her eyes, allowing the sound to guide her inward. Suddenly, she saw her younger self— a little girl, twirling barefoot in a field of wildflowers, her hair wild, her face radiant. But then— her mother's voice echoed through the scene. 🗣 "Don't get dirty, Sophia! Be a good girl."

The little girl froze, her joy dimming, her dance stopping mid-spin.

Sophia's heart broke. 💬 "I silenced her. I abandoned her joy."

She stepped into the scene, approaching her younger self. 💡 "It's okay. You can dance again."

The girl looked up, hesitant, tears in her eyes. 💬 "But I wanted to make them proud."

Sophia knelt down, her own tears falling freely. 💡 "You don't have to earn love. You were always worthy—just as you are."

The little girl smiled, tentatively at first, then fully— the pure, unfiltered joy returning to her face.

And in that moment, Sophia felt something inside her unlock— a freedom she hadn't felt in years.

The Inner Child: Keeper of Wounds and Wonders 💙✨

The inner child holds both our deepest wounds and our purest light.

- It remembers the moments we were hurt.

- It remembers the times we felt unworthy.

- But it also remembers our joy, our dreams, our freedom. 💡 "To heal, we must not only face the pain but also reclaim the wonder."

For Numan and Sophia, meeting their inner child was the first step in this reclamation— an act of compassion, forgiveness, and deep healing.

The Power of Reparenting 🌿💡

When we abandon our inner child, we wait for someone else to save them— a partner, a friend, a mentor. But the truth is— 💡 "We are the ones we've been waiting for."

Reparenting means becoming the adult that our younger self always needed.

- Numan realized he could offer himself the love his father never did.

- Sophia understood she could give herself the freedom to be imperfect, to be messy, to be real.

This was empowerment— the shift from waiting for love to becoming love.

The First Steps Toward Wholeness 🎲 🐚

Meeting the inner child is not about fixing them. It's about seeing them. Hearing them. Loving them.

- Numan, for the first time, held space for his emotions without judgment.

- Sophia allowed herself to laugh, dance, and even cry— without needing permission. 💡 "Wholeness isn't becoming someone new. It's remembering who you were before the world told you who to be."

Through their inner child, they began this remembrance.

Closing Reflection: The Child Within 🐵 💗

There is a part of you, right now, still waiting to be seen. A younger version— pure, tender, and full of life.

- Maybe they feel abandoned.

- Maybe they feel unworthy.

- Maybe they're still hiding in the shadows. But they are still there— waiting for you to return. 💡 "Healing is not about becoming whole. It's about realizing you already are—and bringing all the lost pieces back home." 🎲 💗

Chapter 7

The Dance of Shadows and Light ☻ ♡

You Are Not Just the Light—You Are the One Who Holds It All
For so long, we are taught to chase the light—

- To be positive.
- To be good.
- To rise above.

But in that pursuit, we learn to fear the dark—

- Our anger.
- Our shame.
- Our deepest wounds.

💡 "But the path to wholeness isn't about becoming more light. It's about embracing the dark, and realizing it, too, belongs."

This is the dance of shadows and light—where healing truly begins.

Numan: Facing the Anger Within ♭ 🔥

After meeting his inner child, Numan felt a wave of compassion. But what followed surprised him—Rage.

- Rage at his father for the years of emotional suppression.
- Rage at himself for abandoning his feelings.
- Rage at the world for teaching boys to equate strength with silence.

It bubbled beneath the surface, hot and raw, threatening to consume him. 💬 "I'm not supposed to feel this. I'm supposed to heal, not be angry."

But the more he resisted, the stronger it grew. Until one evening, sitting alone, he picked up a pillow, pressed it to his face, and screamed. The sound was primal—years of repressed emotion pouring out in waves. Tears followed the rage—deep, guttural sobs that left him trembling. And then... Stillness. 💡 "I've been carrying this for so long."

He realized then that anger wasn't the enemy. It was the part of him that had been silenced—a messenger, begging to be seen. 💡 "Anger isn't bad. It's the body's way of saying, 'Something needs to change.'"

By allowing it, by holding it with compassion, Numan felt a piece of himself return.

Sophia: The Embrace of Shame 🌸 🦋

Sophia's shadow wasn't anger—it was shame. After reconnecting with her inner child, she expected to feel lighter. But instead, waves of self-judgment rose:

- "You've wasted so much time pretending."

- "You're not strong enough to heal."

- "You'll never be enough."

It was suffocating, like being wrapped in chains of her own making. For days, she avoided it—numbing with TV, scrolling through social media, anything to escape the heaviness. But one morning, while journaling, the words spilled out: 💡 "I hate this part of me. The part that feels unworthy."

She stared at the sentence, heart pounding. 💬 "What if, instead of hating it, I could hold it?"

She closed her eyes, placing her hands over her chest, and whispered to herself: 💡 "Even in this shame, I choose to love you."

Tears fell, but this time, they felt cleansing. In that moment, she realized that shame only thrives in silence and secrecy. 💡 "When brought into the light, it begins to dissolve."

Her shame didn't disappear completely, but it no longer held the same power.

The Dance of Shadows and Light 🌘✨

Both Numan and Sophia were beginning to see the truth— 💡 "Healing isn't about erasing the shadows. It's about learning to dance with them."

- The anger.
- The shame.
- The fear.

All had a place. All had something to teach. The key was not in rejection, but in integration. Because the Psyche within holds it all—the darkness and the light, the pain and the joy, the brokenness and the wholeness. 💡 "You are not just the light. You are the container that holds the entire spectrum."

The Power of Integration 🩹💞

When we stop fighting our shadows, we reclaim our power.

- Numan felt more whole—not because his anger disappeared, but because he no longer feared it.
- Sophia felt lighter—not because her shame was gone, but because she could finally hold it with compassion.

This was true healing—the merging of all parts, the acceptance of all layers. 💡 "The Psyche within is not fractured. It is vast enough to hold it all."

The Light Emerges Through the Cracks 🌸 🌿

There's a Japanese art called Kintsugi—the practice of repairing broken pottery with gold, highlighting the cracks rather than hiding them. 💡 "The piece becomes more beautiful for having been broken."

This is what Numan and Sophia were beginning to experience— Their cracks, their wounds, their shadows—were not marks of failure, but the very places where the light now shined through. 💡 "Wholeness isn't perfection. It's embracing your beautiful, messy, radiant humanity."

Closing Reflection: Loving the Shadows ☯ 💡

We all carry shadows.

- The parts we hide.
- The emotions we suppress.
- The wounds we fear.

But they are not here to destroy us. They are invitations—to go deeper, to love harder, to return home to ourselves. 💡 "When you can hold both your darkness and your light with love, you are free."

Numan and Sophia were learning this dance. And now, dear reader, perhaps it's time to ask yourself— 💡 "What shadow within me is longing to be seen?" 📝 💗

The Liberation of Truth ◊ ♋

Your Freedom Begins the Moment You Choose to Be Fully You We live much of our lives behind layers—

- Layers of expectation.

- Layers of fear.

- Layers of who we think we should be.

But beneath it all, beneath the masks, the wounds, the shadows, is a simple, powerful truth: ♀ "You are already whole. You've just been taught to forget."

The path to freedom is not about becoming someone new—it's about remembering who you've always been. This is the liberation of truth.

Numan: Speaking the Words He Never Could 🗨 🗣

Numan sat in his father's living room, the tension thick, decades of unspoken words hanging between them. His father, Adil, still carried the same stoic expression—rigid, controlled, as if vulnerability was poison. Numan's heart raced. He had practiced this moment in his mind for years. But now, sitting across from the man who had shaped so much of his identity, he realized something profound— ♀ "I'm not here to blame. I'm here to free myself."

With a shaky breath, he began. 🗣 "Dad, I need to say something. Something I've been holding in for too long."

Adil looked up, guarded. 🗣 "I spent most of my life trying to make you proud. Trying to be strong, trying not to feel too much, because I thought that's what you wanted."

A long pause. 🗣 "But it broke me. I lost who I was. And I'm done hiding."

Tears welled in Numan's eyes, but he didn't hold them back. 🗣 "I'm not perfect. I'm not always strong. And that's okay."

His father sat in silence, emotion flickering behind the walls he had built for so long. For a moment, Numan felt exposed, raw—but also free. 💡 "I don't need his validation anymore. I've validated myself."

And in that, he reclaimed his power.

Sophia: Reclaiming Her Voice ✿ 🗣

Sophia stood in front of a small circle of women—a support group she had hesitated to join for weeks. Her palms were sweaty, her heart raced, but for the first time in her life, she wasn't going to hide. She cleared her throat, her voice trembling. 🗣 "I've spent my whole life being who everyone else needed me to be."

The women listened, their eyes filled with empathy. Sophia took a deep breath, feeling the weight of her words. 🗣 "I've been the good daughter, the perfect student, the ideal friend. But in all of that, I lost myself."

Tears welled up, but she didn't hold them back. 🗣 "I'm tired of pretending. I want to be real. I want to be me."

The room was silent, but it wasn't empty. It was filled with the unspoken support of women who understood. In that moment, Sophia felt a shift—a liberation. 💡 "I don't need to be perfect to be loved. I just need to be me."

And with that, she reclaimed her voice.

The Power of Truth 🌸 🔑

The liberation of truth isn't about grand gestures or dramatic revelations. It's about the quiet, courageous moments when we choose to be real.

- Numan, speaking his truth to his father, freed himself from decades of silence.
- Sophia, reclaiming her voice in a circle of women, found the courage to be herself.

💡 "Truth is the key that unlocks the chains we've placed around our hearts."

When we speak our truth, we not only free ourselves, but we also give others permission to do the same.

The Ripple Effect of Authenticity 🦜 💟

Authenticity is contagious. When we choose to be real, we inspire others to do the same.

- Numan noticed that his relationship with his father began to shift. Adil, once stoic and guarded, started to open up, sharing stories and emotions he had kept hidden for years.
- Sophia found that her friendships deepened. The women in her support group began to share their own truths, creating a space of mutual vulnerability and strength.

💡 "When we are authentic, we create a ripple effect of truth and liberation."

The Journey Continues 📝 🌿

The liberation of truth is not a destination—it's a journey. It's a daily choice to be real, to be vulnerable, to be free.

- Numan and Sophia had taken their first steps, but the path ahead was still unfolding.
- They knew there would be challenges, moments of doubt, and times when the old masks would try to return.

But they also knew that they had found something invaluable—their true selves. 💡 "The journey of truth is the journey home."

Closing Reflection: Embracing Your Truth ❋ ♡

There is a truth within you, waiting to be spoken.

- It might be buried beneath layers of fear and expectation.
- It might be hidden behind the masks you've worn for so long.

But it is there, waiting for you to find the courage to speak it. ♀ "Your truth is your liberation. Your authenticity is your power."

Numan and Sophia found their truth. And now, dear reader, it's time for you to find yours. ♀ "What truth within you is longing to be spoken?" ▨ ♡

Chapter 9

The Return to Wholeness 🌿 ✦

You Were Never Broken—You Just Forgot Your Wholeness The greatest illusion we live with is the belief that we are broken. We spend years trying to fix, heal, and piece ourselves back together, but the truth is simpler— 💡 "You were never broken. You only believed you were."

Wholeness was always there, hidden beneath the masks, the wounds, the stories. And now, Numan and Sophia stood at the threshold—not of becoming someone new, but of remembering who they had always been.

Numan: Coming Home to Himself 🦋 💗

For the first time in his life, Numan felt still. Not the stillness that comes from suppression, but the deep, peaceful stillness that arises when there's nothing left to prove. He walked through the park, feeling the breeze against his skin, noticing the way the leaves danced in the wind. 💡 "I've been so disconnected from this."

From life. From presence. From himself. He sat beneath an old oak tree—the same kind he'd sat under as a boy—and closed his eyes. Breathing in, he felt the aliveness in his body. Breathing out, he felt a soft smile forming, not forced, but effortless. 💭 "I'm here. I'm enough. Just as I am."

For so long, he'd believed he needed to achieve, to control, to strive. But in this moment, he realized the truth— 💡 "I am whole, even in my flaws. I am complete, even in my imperfections."

Tears welled, but they weren't tears of pain—they were tears of returning. He was home.

Sophia: Embracing Her Fullness ❀ ☘

Sophia stood barefoot in her living room, soft music playing in the background. For years, she had controlled every part of herself—her body, her emotions, her desires. But now, she let go. She began to move—slowly at first, then freely, her body swaying with the rhythm, untamed, unapologetic. ♀ "I'm allowed to take up space."

Her dance wasn't polished or perfect—it was raw, real, alive. As she spun, memories surfaced—

- Of the little girl who had once danced without fear.
- Of the teenager who had stopped, believing she wasn't good enough.
- Of the woman who had spent years hiding her brilliance.

But now, she reclaimed it all. She placed her hand over her heart, feeling it beat— ♀ "I am here. I am whole. I am free."

In that moment, she no longer needed to perform. No longer needed to prove. She simply was—radiant, complete, and alive.

Wholeness Isn't Perfection 📖 ♀

We often mistake wholeness for perfection—believing that once we heal all our wounds, once we fix every flaw, we will be complete. But Numan and Sophia had discovered the deeper truth— ♀ "Wholeness is not the absence of wounds. It's the acceptance of them."

It's embracing the shadows alongside the light. It's loving the parts that still ache, even as they heal. It's realizing that you were always enough, even in your brokenness. This was the return—not to a perfect self, but to the whole self.

The Integration ❧ ♡

Healing had once felt like a battle—a constant struggle to fix and mend. But now, Numan and Sophia realized that healing wasn't about fighting the broken parts, but about integrating them.

- Numan no longer suppressed his emotions. He allowed them to flow, holding them with compassion.
- Sophia no longer silenced her voice. She spoke her truth, even when it trembled.

They had become the safe space they had once searched for in others. 💡 "Wholeness is when every part of you knows it belongs."

The Ripple Effect of Wholeness 🌀 ✦

When we return to ourselves, we return to the world in a new way.

- Numan found his relationships deepening, not because he was "fixed," but because he was real.
- Sophia noticed strangers smiling at her, as if they could sense the shift within her—the radiance of someone who had come home to herself.

Wholeness ripples outward— 💡 "When you heal yourself, you heal the world around you."

Their presence alone became an invitation for others to return to their own wholeness.

The Sacred Union Within 🖼 ♡

In every human being, there is a dance between the masculine and feminine—

- The doing and the being.
- The strength and the softness.
- The mind and the heart.

For so long, Numan had lived in the masculine—pushing, achieving, controlling. Sophia had lived in the feminine's shadow—pleasing, perfecting, performing. But now, they felt the balance returning.

- Numan softened, embracing his emotions without losing his strength.
- Sophia stood taller, rooted in her power without abandoning her softness.

💡 "True wholeness is the sacred union of all that you are."

Closing Reflection: The Return Home ✳ ☙

You were never broken. You were never lost. You were never separate. You simply forgot. But now, just like Numan and Sophia, you can remember— 💡 "Wholeness isn't something to find. It's something to return to."

It has been waiting for you all along, in the quiet spaces between your thoughts, in the tender places of your heart, in the depths of your Psyche within. You are already whole. You are already free. The journey was never about becoming—it was always about remembering. 📓 ♡

Chapter 10

Awakening the Divine Within ✻ ❧

The Sacred Was Never Outside You—It Has Always Been Within For so long, we search for the divine in distant places—

- In temples and churches.

- In books and teachers.

- In the skies above, believing that divinity is something far away, something we must strive to reach.

But the ultimate truth is simple— 💡 "The divine was never separate. It has always been within you."

Not in a distant heaven, but in your breath, your heart, your very being.

This is the awakening Numan and Sophia had been moving toward all along— the remembrance that they were never just human. They were always something more.

Numan: The Moment of Stillness 📖 ✦

It happened in the most ordinary moment. Numan sat by the river, watching the water flow, the sunlight dancing on its surface. His mind, usually so loud, had grown quiet. There was no striving. No thoughts of healing or becoming. Just presence. 💡 "Is this what peace feels like?"

As he focused on the river, something shifted. The boundaries of his body felt less defined— as if he was no longer separate from the water, the trees, the sky. A deep stillness washed over him, and in that stillness, a profound truth emerged— "I am not just this body. I am not just these thoughts. I am something more."

Tears welled in his eyes, but they weren't from pain— they were from awe. He felt it— not as a thought, but as a living truth: "The divine is not outside me. It is me."

For the first time, he wasn't seeking the sacred. He was the sacred.

Sophia: The Heart's Opening

Sophia had always been drawn to the idea of the divine— but it had felt distant, something outside herself. Until one evening, while meditating in her room, something shifted. Her breath slowed, her body relaxed, and her awareness drifted inward. She placed her hand over her heart, feeling its steady beat. "I've spent so long searching outside myself. But what if it's always been here?"

A warmth spread through her chest— gentle at first, then growing, filling her entire being. It was love, but not the kind that comes and goes. This was infinite, unconditional, eternal. "I am love. I always have been."

Tears streamed down her face, but there was no sadness. Only awe. Only truth. She felt it deeply— "The divine has always been within me. I am not separate. I never was."

In that moment, her heart opened fully, and she became the love she had been searching for all along.

The Illusion of Separation

The greatest lie we've been taught is that we are separate—

- From each other.
- From nature.
- From the divine.

But Numan and Sophia had now seen through the illusion. "We are not drops in the ocean. We are the entire ocean in a single drop."

The separation had only ever existed in their minds— in the layers of conditioning, wounds, and forgotten truths. But beneath all of it, they were already whole, already divine, already free.

The Embodiment of the Divine 🌿 ❀·
Awakening the divine within isn't about transcending the human experience. It's about fully embodying it— bringing the sacred into every moment, every breath, every interaction.

- Numan felt it in the way he listened— fully present, without judgment.
- Sophia felt it in the way she moved— each step, each dance, an act of devotion. 💡 "The divine isn't found in escape. It's found in presence."

They no longer needed rituals or distant teachings to connect. Their lives had become the ritual. Their breath had become the prayer.

The Unity of All Things 🌍 ♡
With the divine awakened within, they saw the world differently—

- The stranger on the street was no longer separate, but a reflection of themselves.
- The trees, the rivers, the sky felt like family— all connected, all alive. 💡 "There is no 'other.' There is only one."

The barriers between self and world dissolved, leaving only unity. This was the ultimate awakening— not just the healing of the self, but the remembrance that there was never truly a separate self.

Living as the Awakened Psyche ❀· ♻
Numan and Sophia had walked through the fire— the wounds, the shadows, the illusions— and emerged not as new people, but as who they had always been beneath it all. 💡 "The Psyche within is the divine within—it was never broken, never separate, never less than whole."

Now, they lived differently—

- From love, not fear.
- From wholeness, not fragmentation.
- From unity, not separation.

Every moment became an act of creation, an opportunity to bring more love, more truth, more presence into the world.

Closing Reflection: The Divinity in You 📝 💗

You have been searching for something— for love, for purpose, for connection. But the truth is— 💡 "What you seek is already within you."

You are not separate. You never were. You are the divine, in human form— messy, beautiful, whole. And the moment you remember that, the moment you feel it in your bones, you become free. 💡 "Awakening isn't about becoming more. It's about realizing you already are everything." 🌸 💗

Chapter 11

Living as the Awakened Self ✳ 🌐

Awakening Isn't the End—It's the Beginning of Living Fully We often think of awakening as a final destination—

- a peak moment of enlightenment

- where everything becomes clear.

But the truth is— 💡 "Awakening isn't where the journey ends. It's where it truly begins."

Because once we remember who we are— once we awaken the divine within— we're called to bring that truth into the world.

Not in grand gestures or perfect actions, but in the simple, everyday moments—

- In how we speak.

- In how we love.

- In how we live.

This is the path Numan and Sophia now walked— the path of the embodied Psyche, where awakening moves from an internal experience to an outward expression of truth.

Numan: Freedom in Expression 🎨 🎨

Numan returned to his art studio— a space he had avoided for months, perhaps years. For so long, his art had been about control— perfect lines, meticulous details, everything structured and safe.

But now, as he stood in front of the blank canvas, he felt something different. A pulse. A freedom. An invitation to create, not from the mind, but from the heart.

He dipped the brush in vibrant colors, letting it flow across the canvas— unstructured, messy, alive. The more he painted, the more he felt— 💡 "This is me. Raw. Unfiltered. Real."

Hours passed in moments. When he finally stepped back, the painting was unlike anything he had ever created—

- Bold strokes.

- Bursts of color.

- Emotion dripping from every line.

But what mattered most wasn't the result— it was how it made him feel. 💡 "This is what it means to live free. To create from the soul, without fear, without control."

And in that moment, Numan realized something deeper— 💡 "This isn't just about art. It's about how I want to live."

Fully expressed. Fully alive. Fully free.

Sophia: Living from the Heart ✿ ♡

Sophia sat in a sunlit café, her journal open, a warm cup of tea in her hands. She watched the people around her— smiling couples, busy workers, a child laughing as he spilled his juice.

But instead of feeling separate, she felt deeply connected. 💡 "We're all part of this. The same divine thread running through us all."

She placed her pen to paper, writing not from the mind, but from the heart. Her words flowed freely— 💡 "I no longer need to perform. I no longer need to be perfect. I am love, and I am here to share that love—not through grand gestures, but through simple presence."

She smiled as she wrote, feeling the truth in every word. Later that day, she passed a woman crying on a park bench. Her old self would have walked by, unsure of what to say or do. But now, she simply sat beside her, offering a tissue, and said softly, 🗣 "You're not alone."

The woman looked up, tears in her eyes, and for a moment, they shared something sacred— a connection without words, a reminder that we are all seen, all held, all loved. ♀ "This is what it means to live awake," Sophia realized. "To be present. To be love. To be human."

The Embodiment of Awakening 📝 ♀

Awakening isn't about escaping the human experience. It's about fully embracing it—

- The joy and the pain.
- The love and the loss.
- The beauty and the mess.

♀ "Living as the awakened self means allowing the divine to move through you in every ordinary moment."

For Numan and Sophia, this wasn't about being perfect. It was about being real— living in alignment with their truth, even when it was uncomfortable, even when it meant being vulnerable.

They no longer sought to control life. They trusted it. They flowed with it. And in that surrender, they found a deeper freedom than they had ever known.

The Ripple Effect of Authentic Living ☕ ✦

Something beautiful happens when we live from our awakened self—
♀ "Our presence alone becomes a gift to the world."

- Numan's art began to touch people deeply, not because it was technically perfect, but because it was honest. Raw. Alive.
- Sophia's vulnerability inspired others to open up, to speak their truth, to love more deeply.

They realized they didn't need to change the world through grand gestures— ♀ "Simply living authentically was enough to create ripples that would reach far beyond them."

Living in Alignment 🌼 ♡

The awakened life isn't always easy. There were still challenges. There were still moments of fear and doubt. But Numan and Sophia now had something deeper—

- A trust in themselves.

- A connection to the divine within.

- A commitment to live from truth, no matter what.

💡 "Alignment isn't about being perfect. It's about returning to yourself over and over again."

Every breath, every step, became a prayer— a living expression of love, of truth, of wholeness.

The Collective Awakening 🌐 ✦

As they walked their paths, Numan and Sophia noticed something extraordinary—

- Others around them began to awaken too.
- Conversations deepened.
- Connections grew richer.
- Hearts opened.

💡 "Awakening is contagious. When one heart remembers, it sparks the remembrance in others."

They realized they were part of something bigger— a collective awakening, a global remembering that was slowly but surely bringing humanity back to its wholeness.

Not through force, but through love. Through presence. Through being.

Closing Reflection: Living Your Awakening ✳ ♀

Awakening isn't a moment— it's a way of life. It's in the way you breathe. The way you speak. The way you love.

♀ "You don't need to wait for the world to change. You are the change. You are the awakening."

Like Numan and Sophia, you have the power to live as your awakened self. To bring your truth into the world. To be the light that guides others home.

♀ "What step can you take today to live more authentically, more fully, more awake?" ▨ ♡

Chapter 12

The Ripple of Awakening

When One Heart Awakens, It Sparks the Awakening of Many
Awakening is never just personal. Though the journey inward feels intimate, quiet, and solitary, "The moment you remember who you are, you create a ripple that reaches far beyond yourself."

Every act of love, every moment of truth, every breath lived in presence vibrates outwards— touching lives, inspiring hearts, and inviting others to awaken too.

Numan and Sophia now stood in this ripple— not as teachers or gurus, but as mirrors— reflecting the truth that lives within us all.

Numan: Becoming the Mirror

Numan never planned to guide others. But as he continued living from his awakened self, people began to notice. His friends saw the shift— the peace in his eyes, the calm in his energy, the depth in his presence.

One afternoon, while having coffee with a close friend, there was a pause in their conversation. His friend looked at him, eyes filled with both confusion and longing. "Man, you seem… different. Happier. Lighter. What changed?"

Numan didn't jump into advice or lessons. Instead, he smiled, took a deep breath, and simply said, "I stopped running from myself. I finally came home."

His friend sat in silence, letting the words sink in. Tears welled in his eyes as he whispered, "I want that too."

In that moment, Numan realized something profound— 💡 "I don't need to fix anyone. I just need to be me. That's enough to inspire change."

He had become a mirror— reflecting what was possible, reminding others of their own wholeness.

Sophia: Leading with Love 🌸 🕊

For Sophia, the ripple effect came through her vulnerability. She started sharing her journey— not from a place of expertise, but from the raw, messy truth of her heart.

At a local community event, she was invited to speak about her path. Standing in front of a small crowd, she felt her hands tremble, her heart race. But instead of hiding it, she spoke into it. 🗣 "I used to believe I had to be perfect to be loved. But I've learned that it's in my imperfections that I've found the deepest connections."

She shared her story— the masks she wore, the wounds she healed, the love she rediscovered within. The room grew quiet, hearts wide open, tears glistening in strangers' eyes.

Afterward, a young woman approached her, tears streaming down her face. 🗣 "Thank you. Hearing your story made me realize I'm not alone in how I feel."

Sophia held her hand gently and whispered, 💡 "You've never been alone. We're all walking each other home."

In that moment, she realized her purpose wasn't to fix others, but to hold space— to be a beacon of love and authenticity, inviting others to do the same.

The Collective Web of Awakening 🌍 💡

Numan and Sophia began to see it everywhere— the subtle but undeniable web of connection that tied everyone together. 💡 "We are all threads in the same tapestry, each of us essential, each of us connected."

Every smile shared, every act of kindness, every moment of truth sent ripples through the web— healing not just individuals, but the collective.

They realized their personal healing was never just about them. It was about the whole. It was about humanity. ♀ "When one person awakens, it becomes easier for others to awaken too."

Living as the Ripple ✤ ℮

The ripple of awakening isn't created through force or control. It flows naturally, effortlessly, when we live in alignment with our truth.

- Numan's art began to inspire others— not because it was technically perfect, but because it was alive with emotion and presence.

- Sophia's vulnerability sparked deeper conversations— people around her began opening up, sharing their truths, and finding their own paths to healing.

They realized that living authentically was the most powerful way to create change. ♀ "The ripple of awakening starts within, but it doesn't end there. It touches everyone we meet, inviting them to remember their own light."

The Infinite Ripple ▨ ✦

The beauty of the ripple effect is that it's infinite. It doesn't stop with one person, one moment, or one act. It continues to expand, reaching places we may never see, touching lives we may never know.

Numan and Sophia understood this deeply. They didn't need to see the full impact of their awakening to know it was real. They trusted that every step they took in truth, every breath they took in love, was enough to create ripples that would change the world.

Closing Reflection: Your Ripple of Awakening ✿ ♡

You are part of this ripple. Every act of love, every moment of truth, every breath lived in presence creates waves that reach far beyond you.

♀ "You don't need to be perfect to make a difference. You just need to be real. To live from your heart. To share your truth."

Like Numan and Sophia, you have the power to inspire, to heal, to awaken. Your ripple of awakening is already in motion. ♀ "What ripple will you create today?" ✎ ♡

The Garden Within 🌿 ✦

You Were Always Whole—You Simply Forgot
There is a place within you that has never been touched by pain. A place untouched by fear, by shame, by the stories you've carried. It is the space you came from— pure, whole, radiant. 💡 "This is the Garden Within."

It has always been there, waiting patiently, through your moments of joy and your deepest pain, whispering softly— 💡 "Come home."

The Return 🗒 💭

Numan and Sophia had wandered far—

- Through the forests of their wounds.
- Through the storms of their emotions.
- Through the deserts of emptiness.

But in the end, their journey wasn't about becoming something new. It was about returning— to the truth, to the light, to the love that had always been within them. 💡 "The garden was never lost. They had only closed their eyes to it."

Now, with eyes wide open, they could see it clearly—

- In themselves.
- In each other.
- In everyone and everything around them.

The separation had dissolved. The illusion had lifted. They were home.

The Garden of Humanity 🌍 ♡

But their journey wasn't just personal. It was a reflection of humanity's journey— a collective forgetting, and now, a collective remembering. 💡 "We, too, have closed our eyes to the garden within."

We have built walls—

- of fear,

- of judgment,

- of separation.

But beneath those walls, the garden still blooms— wild, free, and waiting. Every act of love, every moment of truth, every breath taken in presence is a step back into that garden. And now, humanity stands at the edge—

- Some still lost in the illusion.

- Some with eyes beginning to open.

- Some already walking barefoot through the flowers, calling out to others, 💡 "Come home."

The Eternal Garden 🌿 ✦

The garden within is eternal. It doesn't wither with time, nor does it fade with age. It is the essence of who you are— timeless, boundless, infinite. 💡 "You are the garden. You are the love. You are the light."

Numan and Sophia's journey is a testament to this truth. They wandered, they forgot, they faced their shadows, but in the end, they remembered. And in their remembering, they found the garden within.

Closing Reflection: The Garden Within You ❀ ♡

Dear reader, this journey is not just Numan and Sophia's. It is yours. It is ours. It is the journey of every soul seeking to return to its wholeness.

💡 "The garden within you is waiting. It has always been there. It will always be there."

No matter how far you wander, no matter how lost you feel, you can always return. Close your eyes, take a deep breath, and remember— 💡 "You are already whole. You are already love. You are already home. You are the children of God and The God within." 🖋️🫶

Whether Called or Not called He shall always be there………

The Psyche, God Within. ✽

With love and infinite blessings to you,

From **Nivin, Reshma, Aidan, and Aura**. 💗🙏✦

THANK YOU

9 7 9 8 8 8 9 6 1 0 7 7 4 3